Mathsheets

A collection of 32 useful worksheets on a variety of mathematical topics ages 10-14

Dominic Turpin

ADDITION

Mathsheet 1 Crossnumber Addition
Mathsheet 2 Climbing the Pyramids

SUBTRACTION

Mathsheet 3 Crossnumber Subtraction
Mathsheet 4 Blank Numbers
Mathsheet 5 Hexagon Puzzle
Mathsheet 6 Descending the Pyramids

MULTIPLICATION

Mathsheet 7 Crossnumber Multiplication
Mathsheet 8 In the Clouds Multiplication
Mathsheet 9 Multiplication Messages
Mathsheet 10 The Dice Multiplication Game

DIVISION

Mathsheet 11 Crossnumber Division
Mathsheet 12 In the Clouds Division
Mathsheet 13 Division Messages
Mathsheet 14 Limericks

All NUMBER RULES

Mathsheet 15 Letter Messages
Mathsheet 16 In the Clouds
Mathsheet 17 Missing Numbers
Mathsheet 18 Operation Trails 1
Mathsheet 19 Operation Trails 2
Mathsheet 20 One, Two, Three and More
Mathsheet 21 Odds and Evens
Mathsheet 22 Magic Squares
Mathsheet 23 Century Plus

SPATIAL WORK

Mathsheet 24 Splitting a Square in Half
Mathsheet 25 Splitting a Square into Quarters
Mathsheet 26 Same Area - Different Perimeter
Mathsheet 27 Same Perimeter - Different Area
Mathsheet 28 Isometric Drawing 1
Mathsheet 29 Isometric Drawing 2

GRAPHS & TABLES

Mathsheet 30 Travel Charts
Mathsheet 31 Ticks and Crosses
Mathsheet 32 Compass Directions

Tarquin Group
www.tarquingroup.com

Mathsheet 1

Write the answers to the sums below into the crossnumber squares. The first answers across and down have been filled in for you. There is only one digit in each space.

Across
1. 7 + 14 = **21**
2. 50 + 52
4. 54 + 62
6. 350 + 120
8. 170 + 70
10. 600 + 630
12. 47 + 51
13. 55 + 36
14. 800 + 210
17. 23 + 24 + 24
18. 450 + 564
22. 182 + 74
23. 27 + 28 + 29
25. 38 + 29
27. 29 + 33 + 37
29. 87 + 85
30. 288 + 289
33. 38 + 47
35. 178 + 255
36. 49 + 48

Down
1. 200 + 12 = **212**
3. 180 + 62
4. 46 + 54
5. 62 + 18
7. 510 + 220
9. 320 + 80
10. 5 + 6 + 7
11. 183 + 128
12. 45 + 45
13. 48 + 49
15. 104 + 68
16. 43 + 37
18. 84 + 85
19. 9 + 9
20. 196 + 245
21. 57 + 39
24. 247 + 176
26. 38 + 37
28. 39 + 59
31. 15 + 17 + 19 + 23
32. 13 + 14 + 15 + 15 + 16
34. 8 + 8 + 9 + 10 + 12 + 12

Climbing the Pyramids

Choose a square at the bottom of the pyramid and climb up to one of the two squares directly above it. Add that number to the first number and then continue moving upwards adding the numbers as you go until you reach the top.

For each pyramid, the first aim is to find (a) the largest possible total and the second aim is to find (b) the smallest possible total.

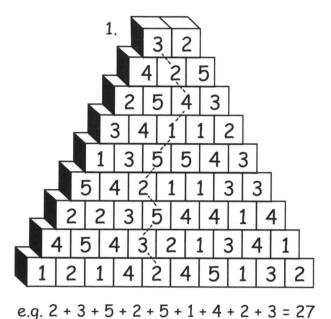

1.

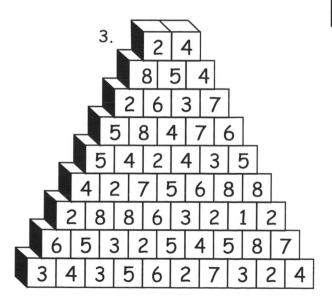

e.g. 2 + 3 + 5 + 2 + 5 + 1 + 4 + 2 + 3 = 27

2.

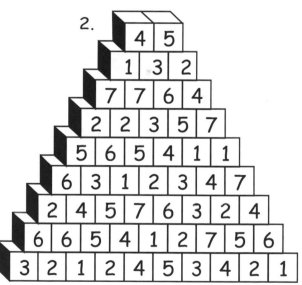

3.

Crossnumber Subtraction

Write the answers to the sums below into the crossnumber squares. The first answers across and down have been filled in for you. There is only one digit in each space.

Across
1. 47 - 23 = **24**
2. 158 - 16
4. 276 - 45
6. 356 - 214
8. 369 - 52
10. 1532 - 410
12. 65 - 28
13. 90 - 39
14. 1252 - 125
17. 898 - 809
18. 1648 - 150
22. 524 - 161
23. 306 - 212
25. 139 - 73
27. 132 - 76
29. 845 - 87
30. 411 - 135
33. 200 - 115
35. 400 - 136
36. 100 - 84

Down
1. 256 - 33 = **223**
3. 287 - 76
4. 357 - 135
5. 79 - 42
7. 489 - 69
9. 188 - 37
10. 99 - 82
11. 136 - 17
12. 83 - 46
13. 127 - 69
15. 335 - 62
16. 135 - 81
18. 316 - 181
19. 168 - 69
20. 920 - 73
21. 124 - 68
24. 365 - 179
26. 100 - 38
28. 200 - 132
31. 300 - 228
32. 400 - 334
34. 500 - 449

Blank Numbers

Place the digits 2, 4, 5, 6 once only into the four blank squares in each subtraction sum. There are 24 different ways that it can be done. Then do the 24 subtraction sums.

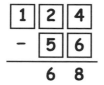

Mathsheet 5

Hexagon Puzzle

Cut out the seven hexagons below and then arrange them into a honeycomb pattern so that a centre hexagon is surrounded by six others with one hexagon at the centre. The puzzle is to arrange them in such a way that whenever one side touches another it shows a sum and its correct answer.

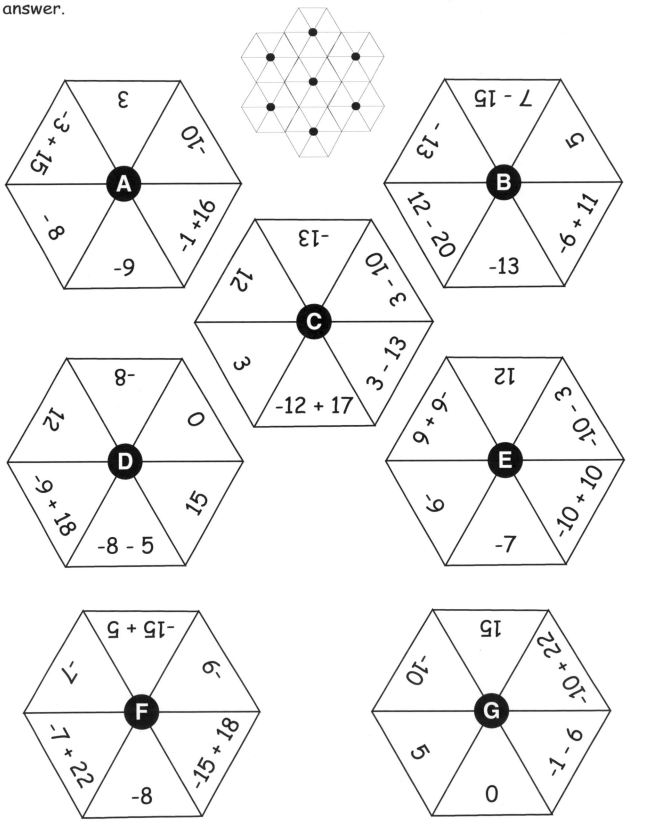

Descending the Pyramids

Start at the top of the pyramid and climb down to one of the two squares directly below it. Subtract that number from the number at the top and then continue on downwards, subtracting each new number as you descend. For each pyramid, the aim is to finish (a) with the largest possible number and (b) with the smallest possible number.

1.

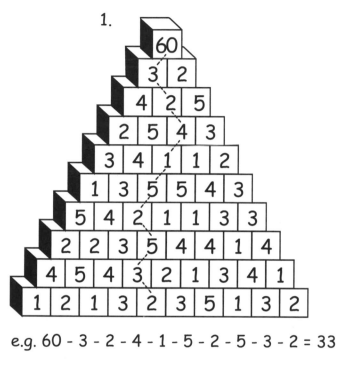

e.g. 60 - 3 - 2 - 4 - 1 - 5 - 2 - 5 - 3 - 2 = 33

2.

3.

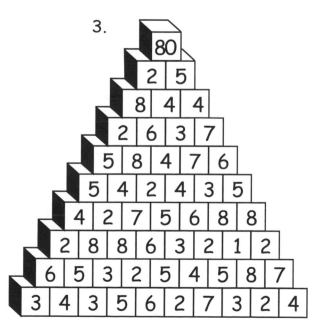

Write the answers to the sums below into the crossnumber squares. The first answers across and down have been filled in for you. There is only one digit in each space.

Across
1. 6 x 2 = **12**
2. 12 x 9
4. 133 x 2
6. 30 x 7
8. 70 x 3
10. 581 x 10
12. 4 x 11
13. 7 x 5
14. 101 x 10
17. 25 x 2
18. 351 x 3
22. 23 x 5
23. 17 x 4
25. 27 x 2
27. 8 x 3
29. 416 x 2
30. 83 x 3
33. 3 x 31
35. 116 x 7
36. 9 x 11

Down
1. 51 x 2 = **102**
3. 414 x 2
4. 40 x 5
5. 18 x 5
7. 11 x 10
9. 50 x 3
10. 9 x 6
11. 5 x 50
12. 10 x 4
13. 5 x 7
15. 11 x 11
16. 20 x 4
18. 76 x 2
19. 28 x 2
20. 97 x 4
21. 25 x 3
24. 162 x 2
26. 2 x 21
28. 7 x 7
31. 6 x 8
32. 13 x 7
34. 3 x 13

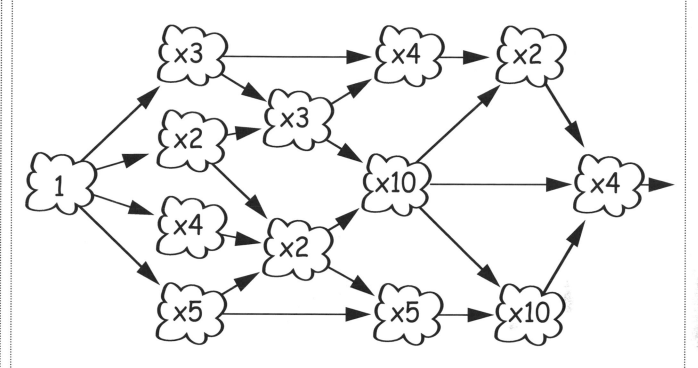

1. Write out a route through the clouds that produces each of the answers below.   e.g. 288 = 1 x 3 x 3 x 4 x 2 x 4

a. 240 = ...

b. 1000 = ...

c. 160 = ...

d. 640 = ...

e. 3600 = ...

f. 800 = ...

2. List some other routes with an answer between 1000 and 2000.

....

....

Mathsheet 9

Multiplication Messages

Start at the cell labelled (1) and work out the sum underneath. Then move to the cell which has that answer at the top and write down the letter in that cell. Then work out the next answer and so continue from cell to cell collecting letters. They will eventually give you a message and return you to your start cell. The other messages start at (2) and (3).

28 (1) 2 x 3	14 S 11 x 1	94 (3) 17 x 2	27 E 19 x 1	57 A 37 x 1	12 E 11 x 2	87 O 36 x 2	80 P 27 x 3	20 B 13 x 1
84 (2) 11 x 3	51 I 14 x 5	35 P 7 x 1	96 T 31 x 3	42 T 6 x 10	■	74 K 33 x 3	32 T 6 x 6	98 I 41 x 2
24 E 5 x 5	58 U 23 x 3	63 A 22 x 4	21 O 1 x 17	78 S 22 x 3	■	16 I 3 x 6	85 E 47 x 2	49 E 5 x 9
45 O 8 x 7	90 I 50 x 2	36 H 3 x 13	■	46 S 16 x 3	40 A 10 x 2	■	7 Y 2 x 13	100 O 19 x 5
13 L 3 x 3	72 U 15 x 5	82 M 17 x 5	6 U 3 x 5	■	69 L 46 x 2	52 M 18 x 3	■	25 S 1 x 8
92 T 17 x 4	26 O 6 x 5	64 Y 29 x 3	66 T 49 x 2	56 U 6 x 7	10 E 2 x 2	81 L 43 x 2	39 E 10 x 5	76 C 21 x 3
22 T 4 x 4	44 S 23 x 2	86 I 19 x 4	9 E 2 x 7	■	75 C 19 x 3	15 S 4 x 3	93 A 37 x 2	11 T 7 x 3
48 U 13 x 4	37 N 21 x 4	50 S 7 x 7	95 N 16 x 6	4 L 7 x 5	99 E 39 x 2	33 S 3 x 9	70 F 16 x 4	88 T 30 x 3
19 T 16 x 2	8 T 10 x 4	34 M 29 x 2	17 H 2 x 5	54 S 17 x 3	30 U 4 x 7	68 I 16 x 5	18 M 6 x 4	60 A 4 x 11

(1) _____

(2) _____

(3) _____

The Dice Multiplication Game

Choose who is to be Player A and who is to be Player B. Throw two dice in turn and multiply the scores together. Colour in that score on your card if it remains uncoloured. The winner is the first to colour four adjoining squares in a column, a row or a diagonal.

Player A

4	8	15	16	30	20	9	2
24	5	6	3	18	25	1	10
12	36	4	6	12	20	24	2
9	18	12	4	20	15	8	9

Player B

12	1	8	9	15	36	18	2
3	10	16	30	15	4	12	5
6	20	24	12	25	10	2	18
4	8	10	3	6	15	16	6

Crossnumber Division

Write the answers to the sums below into the crossnumber squares. The first answers across and down have been filled in for you. There is only one digit in each space.

Across
1. $40 \div 2 =$ **20**
2. $28 \div 2$
4. $72 \div 3$
8. $75 \div 5$
10. $393 \div 3$
12. $48 \div 4$
14. $100 \div 5$
15. $63 \div 3$
16. $142 \div 2$
18. $888 \div 2$
20. $213 \div 3$
21. $128 \div 4$
23. $296 \div 2$
27. $102 \div 3$
28. $104 \div 2$
29. $92 \div 4$
30. $1880 \div 2$
31. $110 \div 5$
32. $108 \div 3$

Down
1. $60 \div 3 =$ **20**
3. $82 \div 2$
5. $120 \div 3$
6. $330 \div 3$
7. $230 \div 10$
9. $204 \div 4$
10. $55 \div 5$
11. $170 \div 10$
13. $120 \div 5$
14. $486 \div 2$
15. $2870 \div 10$
17. $17800 \div 100$
19. $155 \div 5$
22. $888 \div 4$
24. $852 \div 2$
25. $1490 \div 10$
26. $9320 \div 10$
28. $50000 \div 100$

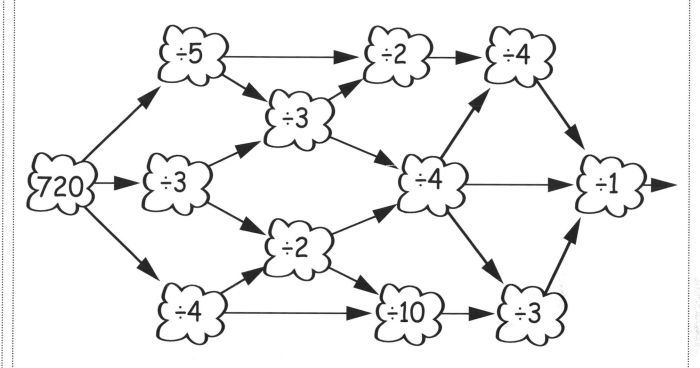

1.   Write out a route through the clouds that produces each of the answers below.   e.g. 18 = 720 ÷ 5 ÷ 2 ÷ 4 ÷ 1

a.   5 = ...

b.   6 = ...

c.   12 = ...

d.   4 = ...

e.   10 = ...

f.   20 = ...

2.   Write out the route that gives the highest possible answer and one of the two routes with the lowest possible answer.

Highest ....

Lowest ....

Mathsheet 13

Division Messages

Start at the cell labelled (1) and work out the sum underneath. Then move to the cell which has that answer at the top and write down the letter in that cell. Then work out the next answer and so continue from cell to cell collecting letters. They will eventually give you a message and return you to your start cell. The other messages start at (2) and (3).

13	12	51	30	92	10	37	35	32
(1)	G	(2)	T	(3)	I	E	O	N
$6 \div 2$	$22 \div 2$	$30 \div 2$	$200 \div 2$	$156 \div 3$	$24 \div 3$	$265 \div 5$	$78 \div 3$	$62 \div 2$
43	25	55	73	22	59	■	42	47
N	W	D	Y	A	O	■	A	E
$102 \div 2$	$68 \div 2$	$355 \div 5$	$240 \div 3$	$99 \div 3$	$198 \div 2$	■	$88 \div 2$	$147 \div 3$
44	60	9	18	36	2	56	■	6
N	W	S	D	I	A	E	■	I
$100 \div 2$	$350 \div 5$	$10 \div 10$	$57 \div 3$	$96 \div 2$	$40 \div 2$	$243 \div 3$	■	$21 \div 3$
8	86	29	72	■	16	23	45	57
D	V	I	F	■	E	I	V	H
$24 \div 4$	$384 \div 4$	$92 \div 2$	$117 \div 3$	■	$80 \div 2$	$48 \div 2$	$87 \div 3$	$112 \div 2$
17	62	33	66	3	97	91	96	14
R	R	R	T	D	E	T	E	D
$72 \div 4$	$122 \div 2$	$82 \div 2$	$216 \div 4$	$10 \div 2$	$460 \div 5$	$240 \div 4$	$380 \div 4$	$39 \div 3$
20	81	26	100	■	41	63	4	61
R	S	R	H	■	I	S	V	Y
$28 \div 2$	$291 \div 3$	$54 \div 2$	$32 \div 2$	■	$96 \div 3$	$177 \div 3$	$20 \div 2$	$220 \div 4$
28	49	15	95	39	99	50	80	21
I	N	S	T	F	L	O	S	H
$90 \div 2$	$182 \div 2$	$63 \div 3$	$171 \div 3$	$148 \div 4$	$258 \div 3$	$90 \div 3$	$198 \div 3$	$88 \div 4$
54	5	48	34	7	71	1	46	27
O	I	O	O	N	I	H	S	D
$189 \div 3$	$12 \div 3$	$172 \div 4$	$51 \div 3$	$24 \div 2$	$144 \div 2$	$20 \div 10$	$72 \div 2$	$84 \div 3$
31	53	■	24	52	19	70	40	11
G	R	■	S	T	F	A	R	I
$69 \div 3$	$47 \div 1$	■	$84 \div 2$	$186 \div 3$	$70 \div 2$	$219 \div 3$	$50 \div 2$	$36 \div 4$

(1) _____

(2) _____

(3) _____

There was a young man from the Humber,
Who woke up one day from his slumber,
'This puzzle' said he,
'Will be clear as can be,
When I've coloured in every odd number'.

Work out the answer to each of the calculations in the squares. Shade all the squares with an odd answer one colour, and those with an even answer a different colour. The resulting shading gives a word.

Grid 1:

7+6		5x3
	13-2	
98-77		56-33
	8x2	
28÷4		22÷2
	12+13	
29-12		22+22
	12÷3	
9x5		7x10
	37+31	

Grid 2:

	22+9	
7x7		41-14
	24÷3	
32-13		5x11
	82-38	
45÷3		35+16
	44+18	
66-19		3x9
	3x13	
54÷2		56+27

Grid 3:

51-16		48+47
	15x5	
44+19		56÷4
	81-77	
3x7		56+38
	75÷5	
9x9		2x9
	77-29	
84-15		74÷2
	77+16	

Grid 4:

	48+63	
54÷6		11x7
	100-45	
85+85		90-52
	56+65	
8x8		96÷4
	13x5	
82+18		80-36
	91÷7	
70-64		6x10

Now here is the start of another limerick for you to complete:

There was a young girl from the coast,
Who claimed she was brighter than most,

Mathsheet 15

Work out the answers to each of these calculations and write them next to the questions.

Then change the answers into letters using the following code
A = 1, B = 2, C = 3 etc. . . . . . . all the way up to Y = 25, Z = 26.

The first two letters of the first message have been done for you.

1.

7 + 6	13	M
12 - 11	1	A
5 x 4		
4 x 2		
10 - 5		
20 - 7		
6 ÷ 6		
20 x 1		
18 ÷ 2		
20 - 17		
10 + 9		
3 x 3		
12 + 7		
17 - 10		
6 x 3		
50 ÷ 10		
20 - 19		
40 - 20		

2.

19 + 4		
9 - 4		
21 - 18		
30 ÷ 2		
12 + 1		
20 - 15		
10 x 2		
5 x 3		
22 - 3		
18 ÷ 6		
8 + 0		
7 + 8		
22 - 7		
5 + 7		
16 - 15		
20 x 1		
7 + 7		
15 - 6		
18 - 4		
10 ÷ 2		

3.

15 - 6		
27 - 7		
5 + 4		
18 + 1		
11 + 9		
10 - 1		
20 - 7		
5 ÷ 1		
13 + 7		
5 x 3		
21 ÷ 3		
30 ÷ 2		
24 ÷ 3		
15 x 1		
8 + 5		
14 - 9		

In the Clouds

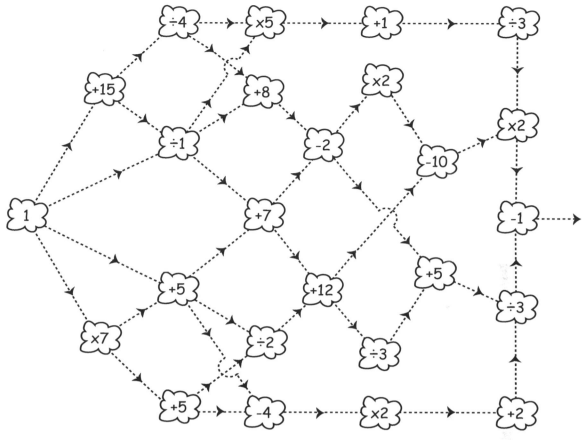

1.   Write out a route through the clouds that produces each of the answers below.   e.g. 47 = 1 x 7 + 5 + 7 - 2 x 2 - 10 x 2 - 1

a.   **3** = _____

b.   **7** = _____

c.   **19** = _____

d.   **4** = _____

e.   **15** = _____

2.   Write out three other routes that give whole number answers larger than 7 and smaller than 20.

a. _____

b. _____

c. _____

Mathsheet 17

Find the number that should replace each letter to make each of the calculations correct.

```
   1 6          4 b          c 7
 + a 3        - 2 7        + 2 4
 ------       ------       ------
   4 9          2 1          6 1
```

```
   8 2          3 e          9 f
 - 2 d        + e 8        - 7 6
 ------       ------       ------
   5 7          7 1          1 7
```

```
  1 4 g         2 7 2        6 j j
 +2 5 6       - 1 h 5      - 1 7 6
 ------       ------       ------
  4 0 3         1 0 7        4 4 6
```

```
  4 8 k        m m 6        6 7 n
 +k 3 k       +7 5 m       +n 7 9
 ------       ------       ------
 1 0 2 0      1 4 2 2      1 1 5 3
```

a =   d =   g =   k =

b =   e =   h =   m =

c =   f =   j =   n =

The rules shown on the sides of the honeycomb have to be used as you move downwards from one hexagon to another joined to it. If one of the two possible answers is correct the trail continues, perhaps to the bottom.
The trail starting with 9 is given and it reaches a dead end at 64. Find the other seven trails starting from the hexagons in the top row.

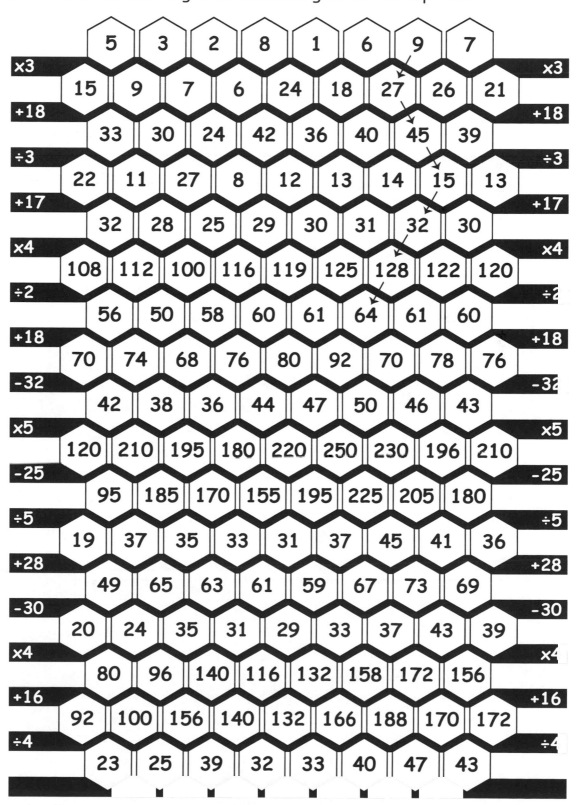

The rules shown on the sides of the honeycomb have to be used as you move downwards from one hexagon to another joined to it. If one of the two possible answers is correct the trail continues, perhaps to the bottom. The trail starting with 9 is given and it reaches a dead end at 21. Find the other seven trails starting from the hexagons in the top row.

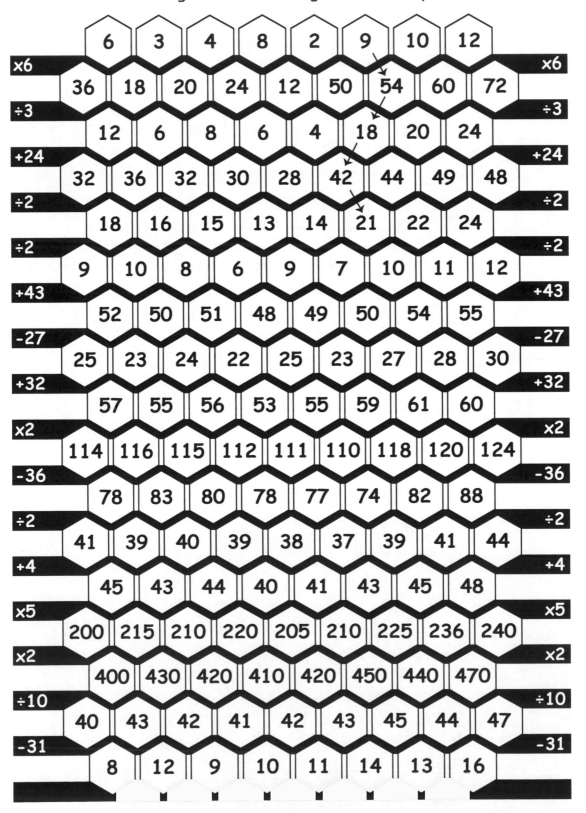

One, Two, Three and More

Starting with 1 each time and using numbers in ascending order (i.e. 2 must follow 1 and 3 must follow 2 etc.) use as few numbers as possible to create calculations with all the answers from 1 to 20.

$1 = 1 + 2 \div 3$

$2 = 1 \times 2$

$3 = 1 + 2$

$4 =$

$5 =$

$6 =$

$7 =$

$8 =$

$9 =$

$10 =$

$11 =$

$12 =$

$13 =$

$14 =$

$15 =$

$16 =$

$17 =$

$18 =$

$19 =$

$20 =$

Work out the answer to each of the calculations in the squares below. Shade all the squares which have an odd answer in one colour, and those which have an even answer in a second colour. You should see a word clearly spelt out.

Block 1

7x3		30÷2
	92-29	
50-17		4x14
	6x9	
28÷4		3x25
	17x3	
7x4		100-19
	24x3	
84÷4		16+17
	7x7	

Block 2

	48+48	
9x5		45÷3
	56-38	
52+51		33÷3
	93-12	
15÷3		9x3
	70-56	
11x9		99-72
	29+21	
99-80		63+72

Block 3

6x15		9x4
	3x13	
85-27		36÷2
	63+58	
12x2		65-37
	82-37	
8x3		32+18
	21÷3	
5x20		12x3
	65-38	

Block 4

	105÷3	
7x5		77-18
	71-69	
91-16		50÷2
	59+58	
9x7		94-65
	76-74	
11x3		16x2
	99-87	
17+76		12x6

Now work out the answer to each of the calculations in the triangles below. Shade all the triangles which have an odd answer one colour and those which have an even answer a second colour. What can you see?

12x5	68+76	57÷3	83-49	80-37	18x3	10x4	24x2
94-38	6x6	105-8	90-42	43+68	84÷7	47-29	72÷9
52-27	85-16	13x5	11x7	49÷7	85÷5	9x13	81÷9
45+45	15x3	64-49	98÷2	91+92	7x9	56+37	57-39

A magic square is an arrangement of numbers so that every row, column and diagonal comes to the same total, called the 'magic total'.

1. Complete these three magic squares using the numbers 1 to 9 once each and then complete the two sentences below.

	7	2
	5	
8		4

1	5	9
		2

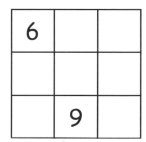

6		
	9	

a. The middle number in each square is ....

b. The magic total for each square is ....

2. Now use the numbers from 3 to 11, once each.

8		
3	7	
		6

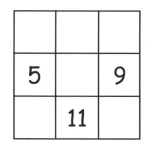

5		9
	11	

	5	10
4		

a. The middle number in each square is ....

b. The magic total for each square is ....

3. Now use the odd numbers from 1 to 17, once each.

7		15
3		11

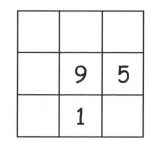

	9	5
	1	

11		
	5	

a. The middle number in each square is ....

b. The magic total for each square is ....

Mathsheet 23

Go to the start square and moving horizontally or vertically, but not diagonally, move to an adjoining square with an answer greater than 100. Then move to another square where the answer is greater than a century and so on until you reach one of the exits. Colour your trail and then start again at the start square. This time move in the same way but only between squares where the answer lies between 50 and 100. Go on until you reach another exit and then colour this trail with a second colour.

START	15 x 7	40 + 70	138 - 36	420 ÷ 2	47 + 47	50 x 2	315 - 251	8 x 6	
18 x 3	16 x 3	121 - 34	29 + 19	21 x 5	100 - 19	81 ÷ 3	200 ÷ 5	52 + 47	A
13 + 39	121 - 25	18 x 2	236 - 142	78 + 24	21 + 76	26 x 4	172 - 65	666 ÷ 6	
73 - 49	102 ÷ 2	213 ÷ 3	98 ÷ 2	200 - 95	176 ÷ 2	61 + 52	200 - 125	211 - 103	
53 + 62	6 x 8	35 x2	450 ÷ 10	312 ÷ 3	136 - 46	18 x 6	149 - 50	17 x 7	
8 x 8	146 - 60	32 + 39	256 - 139	12 x 9	51 + 41	65 + 39	129 ÷ 3	357 - 219	
177 ÷ 3	17 + 18	22 x 2	600 ÷ 5	34 + 14	72 ÷ 2	1010 ÷ 10	38 + 61	85 + 27	
71 + 28	129 - 31	16 x 3	35 x 3	56 + 57	10 x 11	150 - 47	7 x 7	15 x 8	
53 + 54	92 - 33	450 ÷ 5	79 - 37	970 ÷ 10	148 + 84	19 x 5	74 + 17	521 - 408	
100 - 51	104 ÷ 4	16 + 57	160 ÷ 4	99 ÷ 3	151 - 41	32 + 17	12 x 6	420 ÷ 4	B
37 x 2	68 + 33	9 x 6	66 - 13	23 + 46	3 x 10	372 ÷ 6	156 - 65	6 x 5	

D (left side, row 9)

C (bottom)

Splitting a Square in Half

Using the given diagonal line, split a square into equal halves in as many different ways as you can. Use straight lines only and each line must begin and end at a dot. Note that there are no dots at the corners.

One has been done for you.

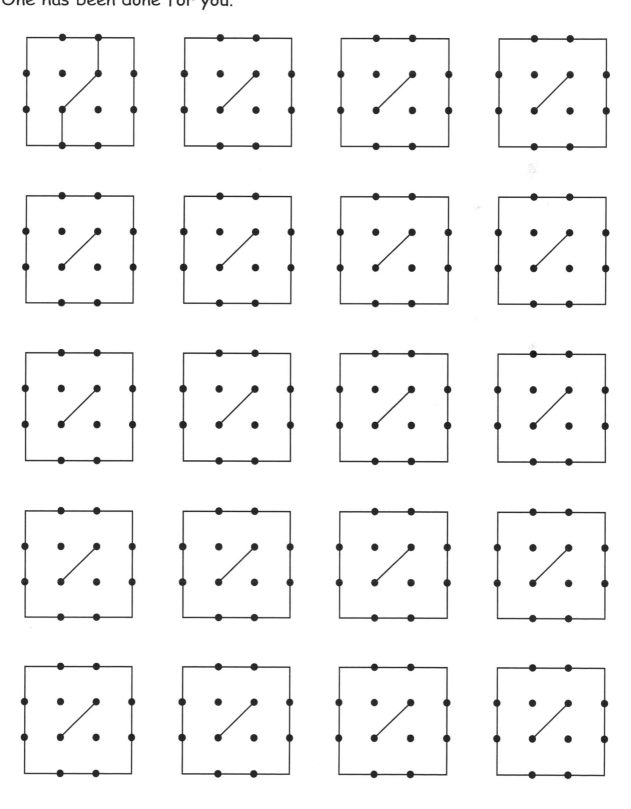

Mathsheet 25

Splitting a Square into Quarters

Using the two given crosses illustrated, split a square into equal quarters in as many different ways as you can. Use straight lines only and each line must begin and end at a dot. Note that there are no dots at the corners.

One using each cross has been done for you.

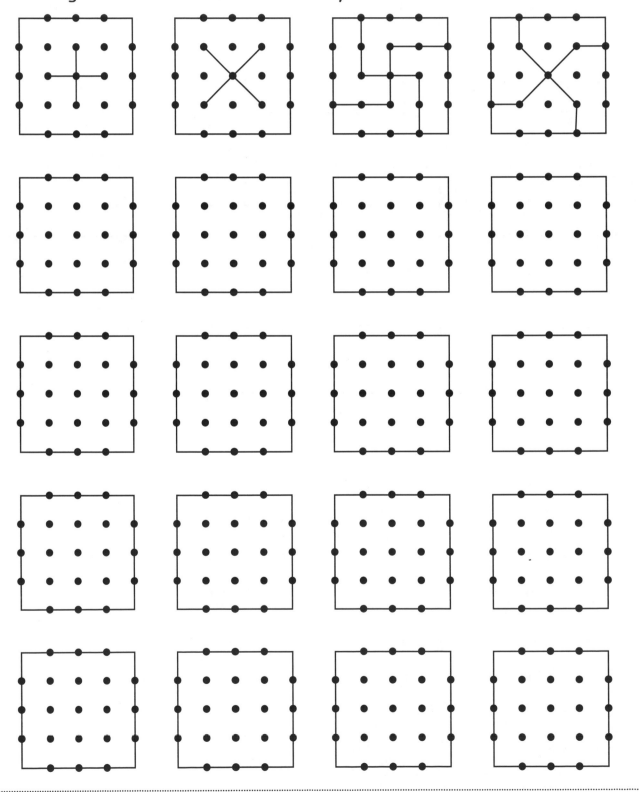

Same Area - Different Perimeter

Draw as many different shapes as you can with their sides on the lines of the 10mm grid below so that each has an area of 5 square cm. Then find the perimeter of each by counting edges. Note that squares must join each other along a side not just at corners.

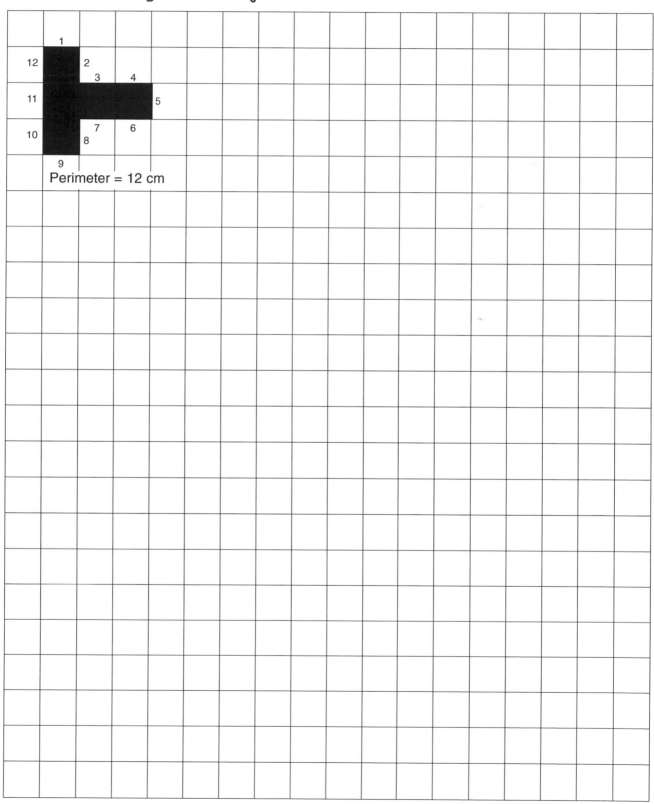

Perimeter = 12 cm

Same Perimeter - Different Area

Draw as many different shapes as you can with their sides on the lines of the 10mm grid below so that each has a perimeter of 12cm. Then find the area of each by counting squares. Note that squares must join each other along a side not just at corners.

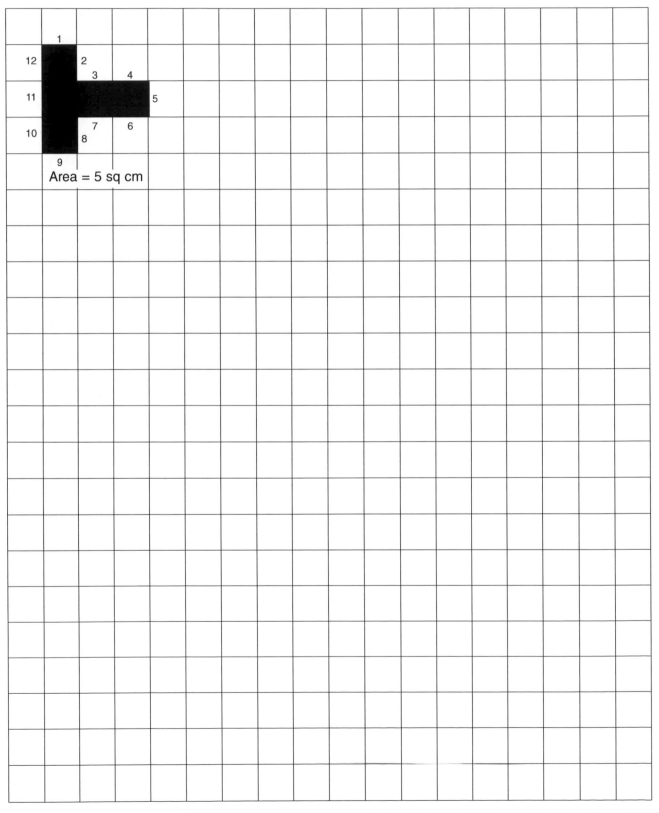

Area = 5 sq cm

Isometric Drawing 1

Carefully copy these eight drawings of three-dimensional objects on to the isometric dotty paper at the centre.

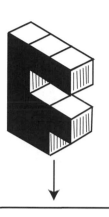 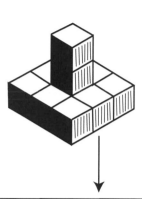 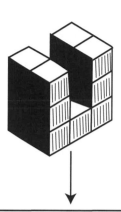 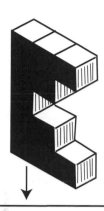

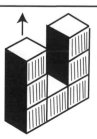  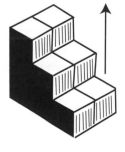 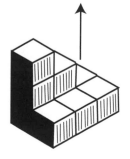

Carefully copy these eight drawings of three-dimensional objects on to the isometric dotty paper at the centre.

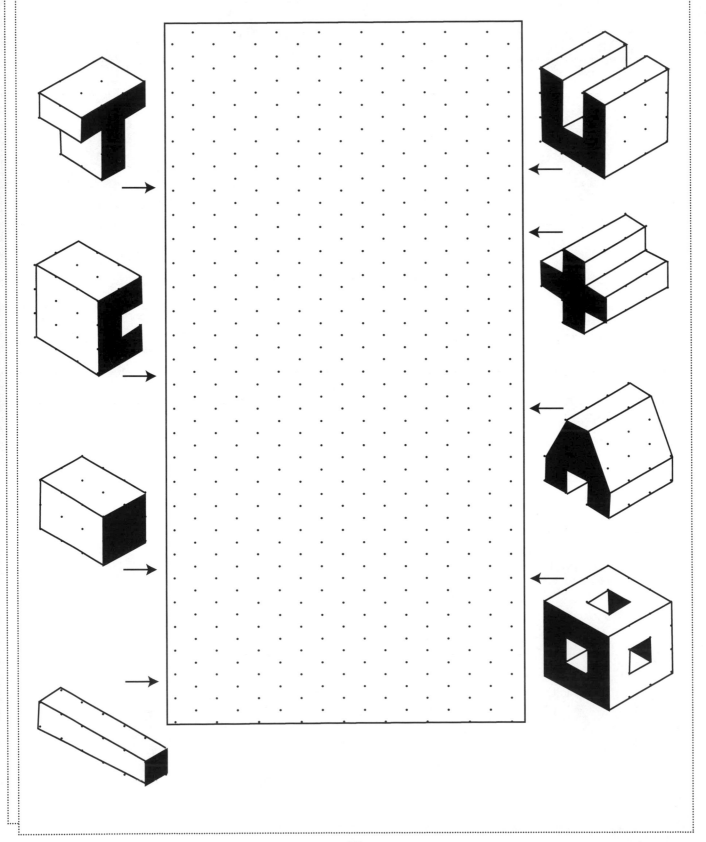

All the distances between the places on this travel chart are given in miles. Use the chart to find the length of each of the twelve journeys shown below.

Birmingham	Bristol	Cardiff	Carmarthen	Gloucester	London	Newcastle	Nottingham	Oxford	Portsmouth	Southampton
88										
106	44									
169	107	67								
54	36	61	124							
120	120	152	215	102						
203	299	317	320	264	285					
53	145	163	226	110	131	160				
68	74	105	168	48	56	257	103			
153	96	155	218	117	74	342	188	84		
134	75	137	200	99	80	324	169	66	20	

1. Southampton ➜ Portsmouth ....

2. Bristol ➜ Carmarthen ....

3. London ➜ Newcastle ....

4. Oxford ➜ Carmarthen ....

5. Nottingham ➜ Cardiff ....

6. Oxford ➜ Newcastle ....

7. Cardiff ➜ Portsmouth ....

8. Carmarthen ➜ Bristol ....

9. Newcastle ➜ Birmingham ....

10. Portsmouth ➜ Nottingham ➜ Newcastle ....

11. Carmarthen ➜ Portsmouth ➜ London ....

12. Gloucester ➜ Birmingham ➜ Nottingham ....

Complete the three charts to show what is true and what is false and then answer the question asked.

✔   Use a tick to show the correct information and

✘   a cross to show false information.

AGES OF FRIENDS

Kate is the oldest of four friends and they realise that they are all of different ages. The chart has already been filled in with this information.

1. Cai is older than Andrew.

2. Saira is the youngest.

How old is Andrew?

	Age 11	Age 12	Age 13	Age 14
Kate	✘	✘	✘	✔
Andrew				✘
Saira				✘
Cai				✘

MORNING BREAK SNACKS

At morning break, five pupils at a certain school noticed that they all had different snacks.

1. Michael and Nia don't like chocolate.
2. Only Nia and Sophie like to eat peanuts.
3. Chris is the only one to like crisps.
4. Claire has milk chocolate every day.

Who was eating fresh fruit?

	Black Chocolate	Milk Chocolate	Potato Crisps	Fresh Fruit	Salted Peanuts
Sophie					
Michael					
Claire					
Chris					
Nia					

THE 100M SPRINT

Six runners in the school 100m sprint all finished and there were no dead heats. The order of finish is shown , 1 to 6, across the top of the chart.

1. Lauren didn't win.
2. Gary came in the top three.
3. Dave wasn't last.
4. Alys came second.
5. Heather beat Gary,
6. Jules wasn't one of the last two.

In which order did the runners finish?

	1	2	3	4	5	6
Lauren						
Gary						
Dave						
Alys						
Jules						
Heather						

Compass Directions

In the town of Compassville, the roads only run in the directions of the eight principal points of the compass N, S, E, W, NE, NW, SE, SW.
Travelling only along roads, give a description for each of the ten journeys between the roundabouts represented by the letters A - R.
For example a journey from E to D should be described as
'Go South to H, then North-West to D' or more concisely 'S to H then NW to D'.

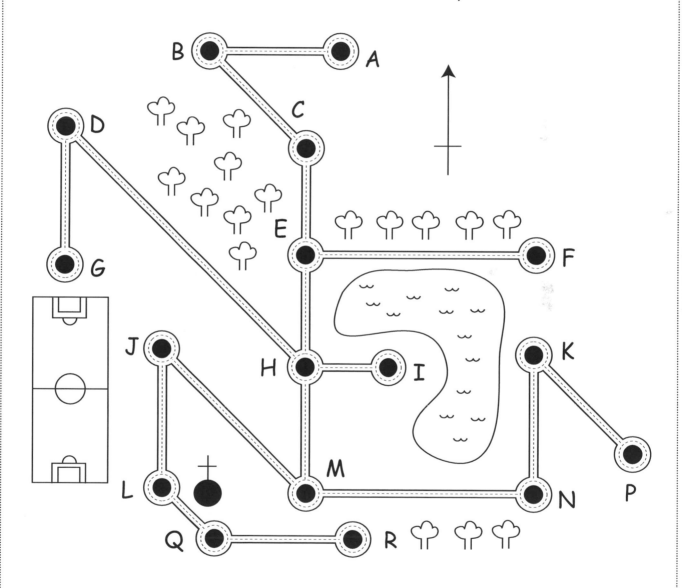

1. From A to C _____
2. From G to E _____
3. From P to N _____
4. From Q to M _____
5. From I to K _____

6. From F to A _____
7. From D to P _____
8. From B to G _____
9. From L to F _____
10. From P to R _____

Mathsheet 1 — Crossnumber Addition

Mathsheet 2 — Climbing the Pyramids

1a. 4 + 3 + 5 + 2 + 5 + 4 + 5 + 4 + 3 = 35
1b. 1 + 3 + 1 + 3 + 4 + 1 + 4 + 2 + 2 = 21

2a. 4 + 4 + 7 + 2 + 5 + 3 + 7 + 3 + 5 = 40
2b. 3 + 2 + 3 + 3 + 1 + 5 + 4 + 2 + 5 = 28

3a. 6 + 5 + 6 + 7 + 4 + 8 + 6 + 8 + 2 = 52
3b. 2 + 4 + 3 + 5 + 2 + 4 + 3 + 5 + 2 = 30

Mathsheet 3 — Crossnumber Subtraction

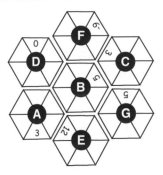

Mathsheet 4 — Blank Numbers

124 - 56 = 68	145 - 26 = 119	156 - 24 = 132
124 - 65 = 59	145 - 62 = 83	156 - 42 = 114
125 - 46 = 79	146 - 25 = 121	162 - 45 = 117
125 - 64 = 61	146 - 52 = 94	162 - 54 = 108
126 - 45 = 81	152 - 46 = 106	164 - 25 = 139
126 - 54 = 72	152 - 64 = 88	164 - 52 = 112
142 - 56 = 86	154 - 26 = 128	165 - 24 = 141
142 - 65 = 77	154 - 62 = 92	165 - 42 = 123

Mathsheet 5 — Hexagon Puzzle

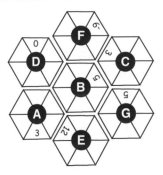

Mathsheet 6 — Descending the Pyramids

1a. 60 - 2 - 2 - 4 - 1 - 4 - 3 - 1 - 3 - 1 = 39
1b. 60 - 3 - 4 - 5 - 4 - 5 - 2 - 5 - 3 - 3 = 26

2a. 72 - 5 - 2 - 4 - 5 - 2 - 3 - 3 - 2 - 3 = 43
2b. 72 - 5 - 3 - 6 - 5 - 4 - 3 - 3 - 7 - 5 = 31

3a. 80 - 2 - 4 - 3 - 4 - 2 - 5 - 3 - 4 - 2 = 51
3b. 80 - 2 - 8 - 6 - 8 - 4 - 7 - 6 - 5 - 6 = 28

Mathsheet 7 — Crossnumber Multiplication

Mathsheet 8 — In the Clouds Multiplication

1a. 240 = 1 x 2 x 3 x 10 x 4
1b. 1000 = 1 x 5 x 5 x 10 x 4
1c. 160 = 1 x 2 x 2 x 10 x 4
1d. 640 = 1 x 4 x 2 x 10 x 2 x 4
1e. 3600 = 1 x 3 x 3 x 10 x 10 x 4
1f. 800 = 1 x 5 x 2 x 10 x 2 x 4
  800 = 1 x 2 x 2 x 5 x 10 x 4

2. There is only one solution but two routes.
  1600 = 1 x 2 x 2 x 10 x 10 x 4
  1600 = 1 x 4 x 2 x 5 x 10 x 4

Mathsheet 9 — Multiplication Messages

1. USE TIMES TABLES TO HELP YOU
2. SET THESE OUT AS SUMS IF YOU CAN
3. MULTIPLICATION TAKES TIME

Mathsheet 10 — Dice Multiplication Game

No solution required.

Mathsheet 11 — Crossnumber Division

Mathsheet 12 — In the Clouds Division

1a. $5 = 720 \div 3 \div 3 \div 4 \div 4 \div 1$
1b. $6 = 720 \div 5 \div 3 \div 2 \div 4 \div 1$
    $6 = 720 \div 4 \div 10 \div 3 \div 1$
1c. $12 = 720 \div 5 \div 3 \div 4 \div 1$
1d. $4 = 720 \div 5 \div 3 \div 4 \div 3 \div 1$
    $4 = 720 \div 3 \div 2 \div 10 \div 3 \div 1$
1e. $10 = 720 \div 3 \div 2 \div 4 \div 3 \div 1$
    $10 = 720 \div 3 \div 3 \div 2 \div 4 \div 1$
1f. $20 = 720 \div 3 \div 3 \div 4 \div 1$

2. Highest $30 = 720 \div 3 \div 2 \div 4 \div 1$
   Lowest $3 = 720 \div 5 \div 3 \div 4 \div 4 \div 1$
   Lowest $3 = 720 \div 4 \div 2 \div 10 \div 3 \div 1$

Mathsheet 13 — Division Messages

a. DIVIDING IS HARD
2. SHARING IS ANOTHER WORD FOR DIVISION
3. TRY DIFFERENT WAYS TO SOLVE THESE

Mathsheet 14 — Limericks

13	11	15		49	31	27		35	75	95		9	111	77
21	16	23		19	8	55		63	4	14		170	55	38
7	25	11		15	44	51		21	15	94		64	121	24
17	4	44		47	62	27		81	48	18		100	65	44
45	68	70		27	39	83		69	93	37		6	13	60

Here's a suggestion of how to finish the limerick, I'm sure you can think of something better!

There was a young girl from the coast,
Who claimed she was brighter than most,
She said 'Three times seven,
Equals two times eleven',
So she's not quite as good as her boast.

Mathsheet 15 — Letter Messages

1. MATHEMATICS IS GREAT
2. WE COME TO SCHOOL AT NINE
3. IT IS TIME TO GO HOME

Mathsheet 16 — In the Clouds

1a. $3 = 1 \div 1 + 7 - 2 \times 2 - 10 \times 2 - 1$
    $3 = 1 \div 1 \times 5 + 1 \div 3 \times 2 - 1$
1b. $7 = 1 \div 1 + 8 - 2 \times 2 - 10 \times 2 - 1$
1c. $19 = 1 + 15 \div 4 + 8 - 2 \times 2 - 10 \times 2 - 1$
    $19 = 1 \div 1 + 7 + 12 - 10 \times 2 - 1$
1d. $4 = 1 + 15 \div 4 + 8 - 2 + 5 \div 3 - 1$
1e. $15 = 1 \times 7 + 5 \div 2 + 12 - 10 \times 2 - 1$
    (The +5 is on two different routes.)

    $8 = 1 + 15 \div 1 + 8 - 2 + 5 \div 3 - 1$
    $9 = 1 + 5 \div 2 + 12 - 10 \times 2 - 1$
    $13 = 1 + 15 \div 4 \times 5 + 1 \div 3 \times 2 - 1$

Mathsheet 17 — Missing Numbers

a. 3	d. 5	g. 7	k. 5
b. 8	e. 3	h. 6	m. 6
c. 3	f. 3	j. 2	n. 4

Mathsheet 18 — Operation Trails 1

5-15-33-11-28-112-56-74-42-210-185-37-65-35-140-156-39
3-9
2-6-24-8-25-100-50-68-36-180-155-31-59-29-116-132-33
8-24-42
1
6-18-36-12-29-116-58-76-44-220-195
9-27-45-15-32-128-64
7-21-39-13-30-120-60-78-46-230-205-41-69-39-156-172-43

The trails stating with 5, 2 and 7 go all the way.

Mathsheet 19 — Operation Trails 2

6-36-12-36-18-9-52-25-57-114-78-39-43-215-430-43-12
3-18-6
4-24-8-32-16-8-51-24-56-112
8
2-12-4-28-14-7-50-23-55-110-74-37-41-205-410-41-10
9-54-18-42-21
10-60-20-44-22-11-54-27-59-118-82-41-45-225-450-45-14
12-72-24-48-24-12-55-28-60-120

The trails stating with 6, 2 and 10 go all the way.

Mathsheet 20 — One, Two, Three and More

$1 = 1 + 2 \div 3$
$2 = 1 \times 2$
$3 = 1 + 2$
$4 = 1 + 2 - 3 + 4$
    $1 + 2 \div 3 \times 4$
$5 = 1 \times 2 + 3$
$6 = 1 + 2 + 3$
    $1 \times 2 \times 3$
$7 = 1 + 2 + 3 - 4 + 5$
    $1 \times 2 \times 3 - 4 + 5$
$8 = 1 - 2 + 3 \times 4$
$9 = 1 + 2 \times 3$
$10 = 1 + 2 + 3 + 4$
    $1 \times 2 \times 3 + 4$
$11 = 1 - 2 + 3 + 4 + 5$
$12 = 1 + 2 + 3 + 4 \div 5 \times 6$
    $1 \times 2 \times 3 + 4 \div 5 \times 6$
    $1 + 2 \times 3 + 4 + 5 - 6$
    $1 + 2 \div 3 - 4 + 5 \times 6$
    $1 - 2 \times 3 + 4 + 5 + 6$
    $1 \times 2 + 3 - 4 + 5 + 6$

$13 = 1 + 2 \times 3 + 4$
$14 = 1 \times 2 + 3 + 4 + 5$
$15 = 1 + 2 + 3 + 4 + 5$
    $1 \times 2 \times 3 + 4 + 5$
    $1 \times 2 + 3 \times 4 - 5$
$16 = 1 + 2 \div 3 + 4 + 5 + 6$
    $1 + 2 \times 3 - 4 + 5 + 6$
$17 = 1 - 2 + 3 + 4 + 5 + 6$
$18 = 1 + 2 \times 3 + 4 + 5$
$19 = 1 + 2 + 3 \times 4 - 5$
    $1 \times 2 \times 3 \times 4 - 5$
$20 = 1 \times 2 + 3 \times 4$

Mathsheet 21 — Odds and Evens

21	63	15		45	96	15		90	39	36		35	35	59
33	54	56		103	18	11		58	121	18		75	2	25
7	51	75		5	81	27		24	45	28		63	117	29
28	72	81		99	14	27		24	7	50		33	2	32
21	49	33		19	50	135		100	27	36		93	12	72

	60		144		29		34	43		54		40		48
56		36		97		48			111		12		18		8
	25		69		65		77	7		17		117	9	
90		45		15		49			183		63		93		18

Mathsheet 22 — Magic Squares

6	7	2
1	5	9
8	3	4

1a. 5

8	3	4
1	5	9
6	7	2

1b. 15

6	1	8
7	5	3
2	9	4

8	9	4
3	7	11
10	5	6

2a. 7

10	3	8
5	7	9
6	11	4

2b. 21

6	5	10
11	7	3
4	9	8

7	5	15
17	9	1
3	13	11

3a. 9

3	17	7
13	9	5
11	1	15

3b. 27

11	13	3
1	9	17
15	5	7

Mathsheet 23 — Century Plus

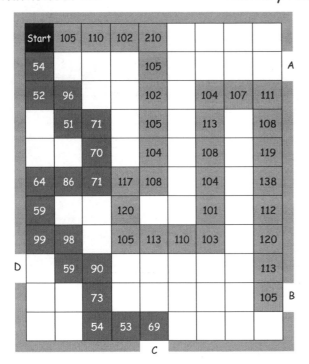

Mathsheet 24 — Splitting into Halves

There are fourteen possibilities but only seven distinct solutions

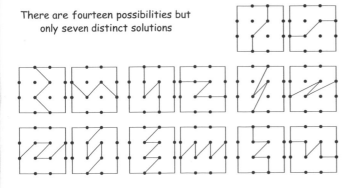

Mathsheet 25 — Splitting into Quarters

There are 29 possibilities but only 15 distinct solutions.

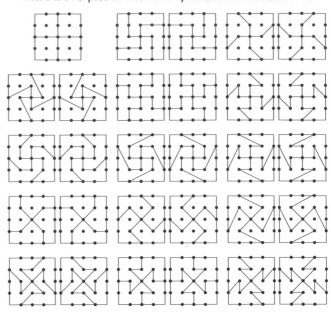

Mathsheet 26 — Same Area

1: perimeter 10 cm

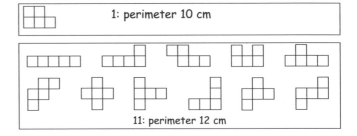

11: perimeter 12 cm

Mathsheet 27 — Same Perimeter

1: area 9 cm²

2: area 8 cm²

4: area 7 cm²

7: area 6 cm²

11: area 5 cm²

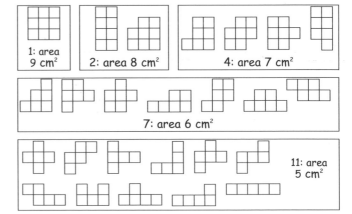

Mathsheets 28 & 29 — Isometric Drawings

No solutions required.

Mathsheet 30 — Travel Charts

1. 20 miles
2. 107 miles
3. 285 miles
4. 168 miles
5. 163 miles
6. 257 miles
7. 155 miles
8. 107 miles
9. 203 miles
10. 188 + 160 = 348 miles
11. 218 + 74 = 292 miles
12. 54 + 53 = 107 miles